AF425789

Latter-day Grooks 4

Bill Wylson

Other Books by Bill Wylson

Hieroglyphs, Golden Plates & Typos

Give Place in Your Heart

Three Minutes Eighteen Seconds

Elder Hammond and The Inspector

A New Earth

The Manger on The Mantle

The Greatest Thing in The World

Latter-day Grooks Vol. I, II & III

Available at:
www.billwylsonbooks.com

First Edition published December 2023
Second Edition published October 2024

White Horse Books
Green Stem Media
South Jordan, Utah 84009

*"If your life is a leaf
That the seasons tear off and condemn,
[He] will bind you with love
That is graceful and green as a stem."*
L. Cohen

www.billwylsonbooks.com
www.greenstemmedia.com

Table of Contents

Introduction:

What is a Grook?

A grook is a short poem with an aphoristic essence. Grooks were initially created by the Danish poet Piet Hein (1905–1996), who wrote over 10,000 in Danish and English. A grook, known as 'gruk' in the Danish language, is a unique literary art form. It is a condensed poetic expression that captures profound meaning in just a few lines. Grooks put pertinent new perspectives on everyday observations, presenting the reader with small instructions on the art of living.

The beauty of this style lies not only in its brevity but also in how it presents wisdom and philosophical insights. Usually expressed in rhyme, these poetry pieces embody cultural or broader life truths. Through simple yet resonant language, grooks encapsulate significant sentiments that make readers deeply contemplate life's various themes and experiences.

Piet Hein, a descendant of Piet Pieterszoon Hein, the 17th-century Dutch naval hero, was born in Copenhagen, Denmark. He studied at the Institute for Theoretical Physics of the University of Copenhagen (later to become the Niels Bohr Institute) and the Technical University of Denmark. Yale awarded him an honorary doctorate in 1972.

One of the author's favorite Piet Hein grooks is entitled:

Small Things and Great

He that lets
the small things bind him
leaves the great
undone behind him.

What is a Latter-day Grook?

As Latter-day Saints, we have a distinctive collection of wisdom and insight exclusive to our faith. It is the revealed truth bestowed upon Latter-day prophets and apostles. This canon is unique and significant within our religious tradition, yet it remains primarily unacquainted to the outside world.

This literature houses profound wisdom concerning life's most significant existential questions. It addresses themes like morality, righteousness, faith, and divinity. The revealed knowledge present within our literature is deeply rooted in our theology.

It is often easier to recall essential writings when they appear in poetic form because poetry resonates with us. We enjoy reading or hearing something that reflects what is in our minds or hearts. I sincerely pray that the message of these Latter-day Grooks will be inscribed onto the walls of our hearts and minds and offer us hope, strength, and encouragement in our effort to resist evil and overcome the world.

"Keep thy father's commandment, and forsake not the law of thy mother:

"Bind them continually upon thine heart, and tie them about thy neck.

"When thou goest, it shall lead thee; when thou sleepest, it shall keep thee; and when thou awakest, it shall talk with thee."

Proverbs 6:20-22.

Perfect Plan

God gave us a plan
for assured success—

His gospel—the great
plan of happiness.

Influencers

When you think about it
It just makes sense—

The devil works
through human agents.

Instill Goodness

Parenthood imposes
a dual responsibility,
(of this, there is no doubt.)

Not just to instill good
in a child's mind but to
also, keep the bad stuff out.

Language is Divine

Some may not comprehend
the meaning behind this message:

True love begins and ends
with a kind and loving language.

No

Sometimes we're confused
by questions that spin
and move though our minds
like a dancer

simply because
we refuse to give in
and won't ever take no
for an answer.

God exists

Evidence on Our Side

You cannot prove God
away from us,
no matter what questions
or doubts you bring.

To know for sure
that there is no God
you must be everywhere
and know everything.

What the World Wants

The world doesn't want
a prophet of light
to tell it to live righteously.

It simply wants to be told
what it's doing is right—
no matter how wrong it may be!

Public Prayer

I have found it is better
to be honest and tender,
whenever we pray aloud,

rather than worrying
over the scurrying
thoughts and minds of the crowd.

The Cost of Peace

The price would be
far less what we'd
pay now than later,

and the rewards we'd
reap would be
indescribably greater.

Watching for Warnings

Some guideposts in life
we see more clearly
after we have passed them,

when, through the promptings
of the Holy Ghost,
we surely could have forecast them.

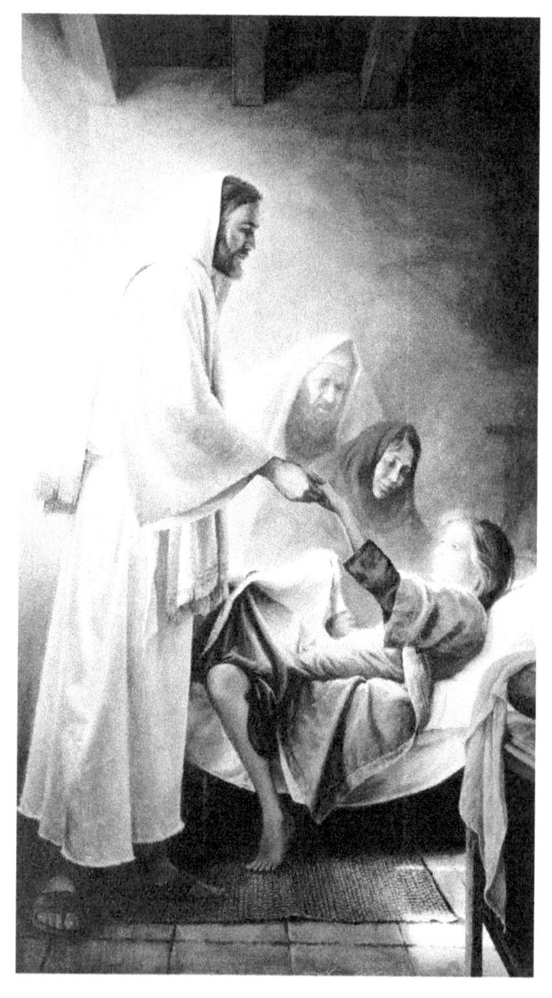

Jairus' Daughter

The deceased young girl
was given new life
raised from death by His command,

and He can raise your world
from its gloom and strife
if you will only take His hand.

Seeking Answers

When the Heavens seem not to speak

through prayerful scripture study
we can attune

our hearts and minds to be fairly
less immune

to the spiritual answers we seek.

Endure with Patience

All that we suffer
and all we endure,
makes us more tender,
more charitable, and pure.

WHAT
DID I
LEARN ?

Adversity

No pain that we suffer,
no bitterness we've tasted,
no trial we've lived through
is truly ever wasted.

Personal Storms

How strikingly beautiful,
in a severe summer storm,
is the temple's floodlit glow,

just as the gospel of Christ
shines so gloriously bright
through storms of personal sorrow.

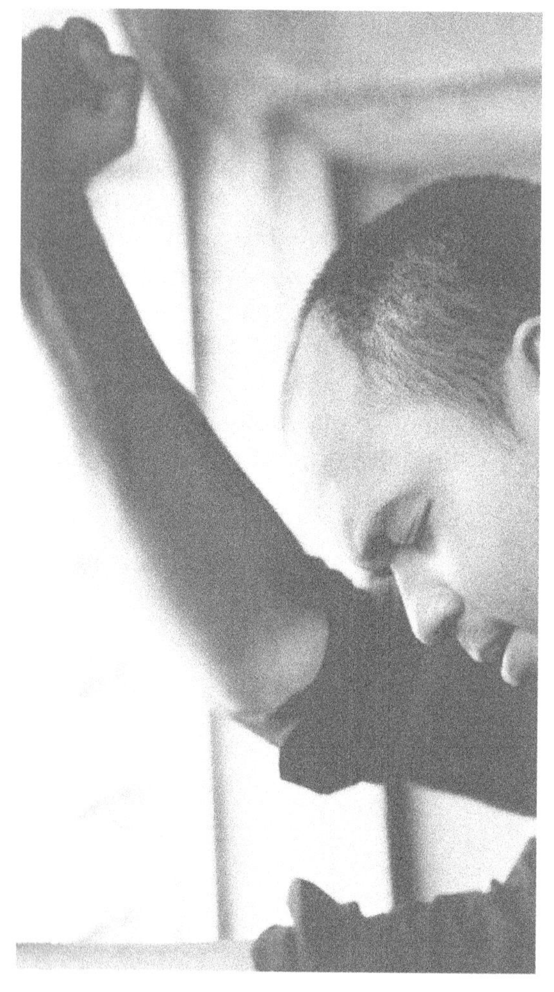

Change and Repent

We need not
forever be

the same person we are
currently.

The Fulness of the Gospel

With an entire keyboard at hand,
how disappointing it must be

that so many settle for the bland,
repeated tap of a single key.

Free Agency

When you can't decide—
you should rejoice;

free agency requires
that we have a choice.

Do Yourself a Favor

When we bring our scriptures
down from their shelves,

the deeper into them
we dare to delve

we'll learn we ought
to keep God's word

simply as a favor
to ourselves.

THANK
YOU

Gratitude

There is
always more

to be
thankful for.

Thy Will Be Done

The key
for you and me
is simply to desire,

whatever the Savior
may require.

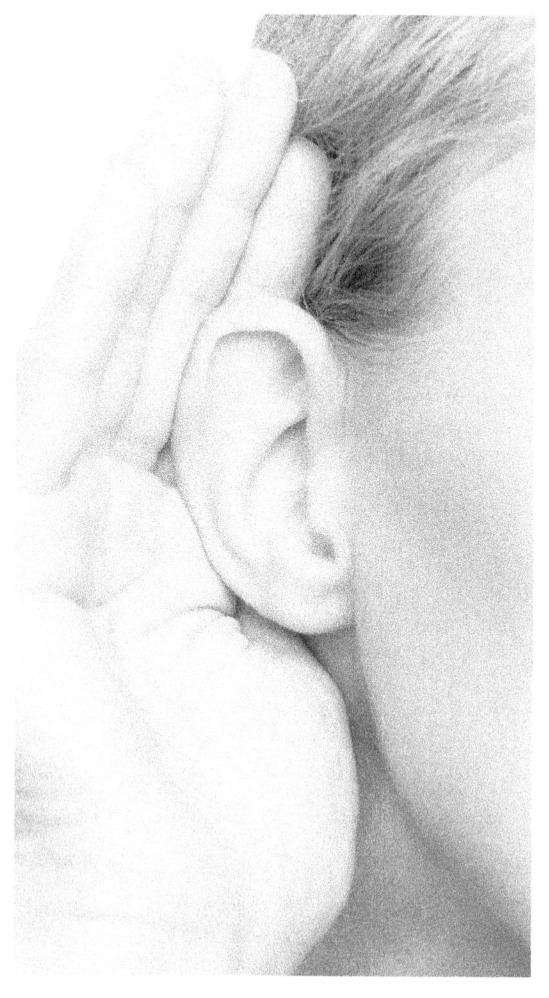

We Don't Need Another Prophet

A prophet has spoken—
a prophet and seer—

what we need now
is a listening ear.

Change is Possible

"Change is a meaningful part of repentance."

Some people are filled
with good intent
their lives to order and re-arrange,

yet still find themselves
helpless to repent
because they're unwilling to change.

Parental Advice

The path of life
can be rough and wild,
an arduous journey
beneath a heavy load.

Don't prepare the path
to suit your child,
but prepare your child
to travel the road.

Social Grook

"He never said a word to me,"
she said with impudent vim,

but does she realize that also she
never said a word to him?

Why Am I Here?

Before I slip
through Death's dark door,

I'd like to know
what Life is for.

Eternal Perfection

The key to achieving
eternal perfection
is found in our own
covenant-connection.

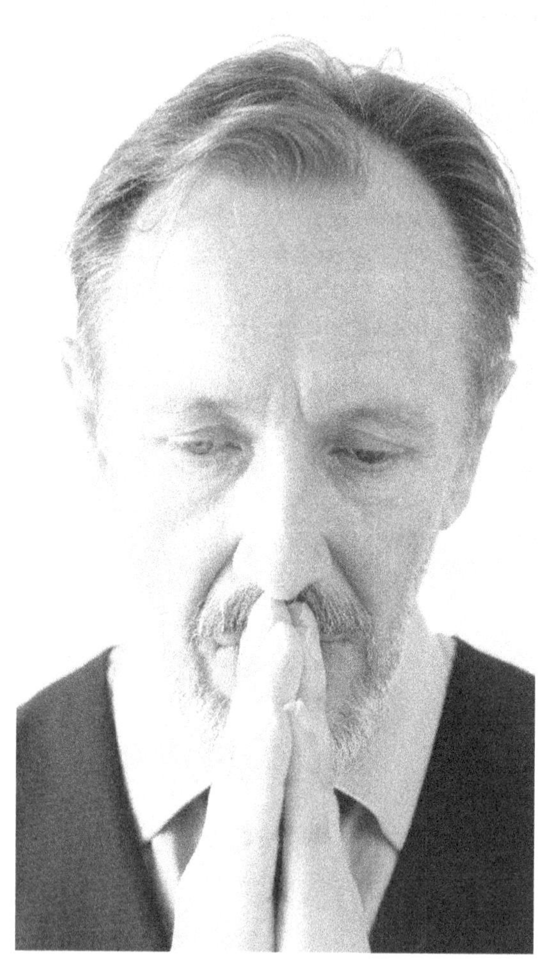

The Cost of Repentance

If the cost of repentance
seems too dear—

forsake your pride,
give up your fear.

Taken for Granted

Our commitment to attend
should be as constant
when the temple is near
as when it is distant.

Life is Eternal

However bad
your earthly circumstance,
however difficult your situation,

remember that this
earthy circumference
is only of temporary duration.

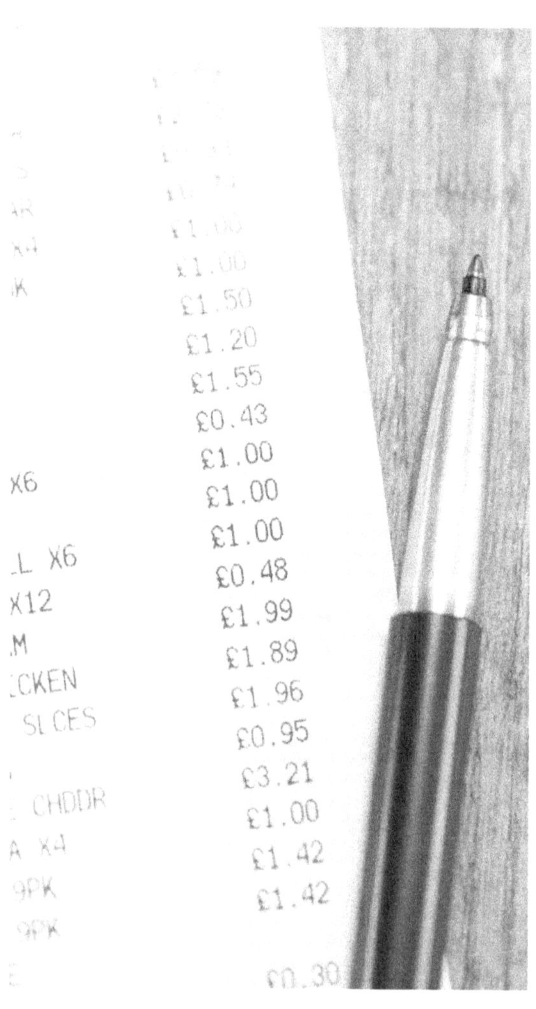
X4
K
£1.00
£1.00
£1.50
£1.20
£1.55
£0.43
£1.00
X6
£1.00
£1.00
L X6
£0.48
X12
£1.99
M
£1.89
CKEN
£1.96
SLCES
£0.95
£3.21
CHDDR
£1.00
A X4
£1.42
9PK
£1.42
9PK
£0.30

Where Your Heart Is

The best gifts of all
are had for a price,

what most we love
comes with sacrifice.

Father of Lies

The pernicious falsehood
that God is dead
is on the very same level

as the malicious doctrine
Satan has spread
that there also is no devil.

Be Slow to Anger

The size of a man
may be had

by the size of the things
that make him mad.

Active Members

The religion of Christ
is not so much
a set of ideas
or philosophies

as it is
a hallowed clutch
or sacred set
of Christ-like activities.

FAITH
SCIENCE

Crossroads

Where true religion
and exact science
come together

there can be
no disagreement,
whatsoever.

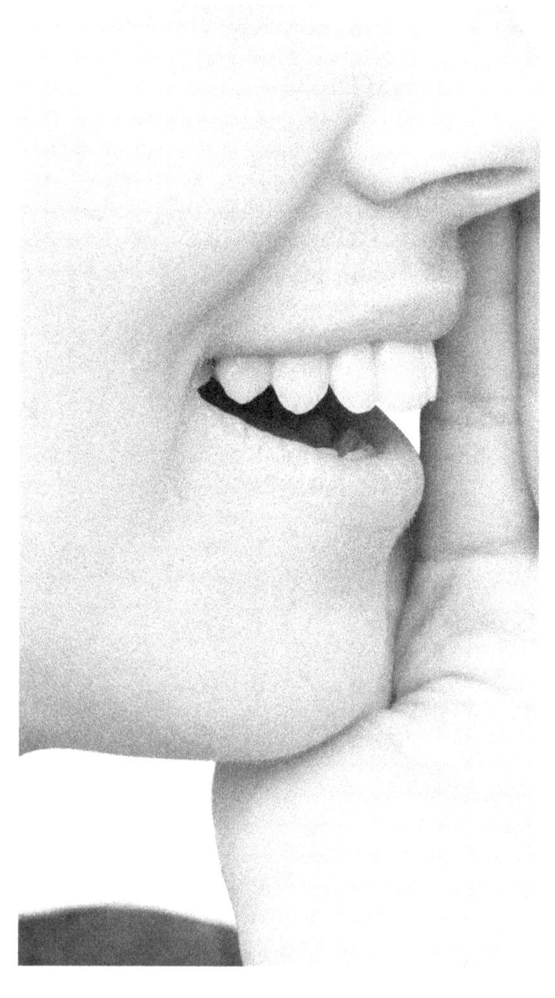

The Soft Answer

"A soft answer turneth away wrath."
Proverbs 15:1

One truth worth remembering—
awfully:

We seldom get into trouble
when speaking softly.

Here and Now

What happens here and now
is important,
that much is an inevitable certainty,

for every day of our lives
is a shortened
little piece of our longer eternity.

The Light of Christ

This wrong-doers truth
 is a subtilty;

the conscience will never
acquit the guilty.

Love at Home

If you want contention to cease
you can make a simple choice—

the tone of domestic peace
is shown in a gentle voice.

The Heaviest Weight

There is no debate,
that the heaviest weight
of this world we all live in

is the crushing load
generously bestowed
by this burden we all call sin.

Blessing Your Marriage

The little storms that afflict
every marriage

dissipate when kneeling
before the Lord.

In the presence of each other,
thank Him for one another,

then invoke His blessings
with one accord.

Now Is the Time

Now is the time
to turn and to go
in the direction that we ought to

before the day comes
when we wonder where
all our precious time has got to.

The Iron Rod

One thing that is desperately needed in this time of frustration and strife, is an iron rod to guide and to lead us on the straight path to eternal life.

Seeking God

The person who seeks
to see God all around him,

in his own subtle way,
has already found Him.

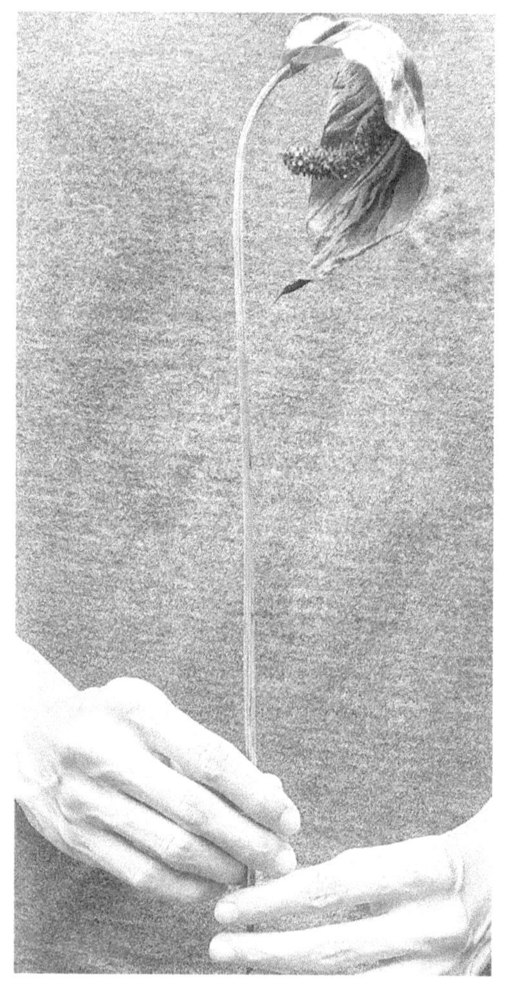

Faith Without Works

Some take the attitude
that, simply having faith,
their salvation is assured.

How absurd!

KJV
HOLY
BIBLE

Unchanging Truth

There is no 'liberal' religion—
I offer you this as proof—

the claim of true religion
must stand on unchanging truth.

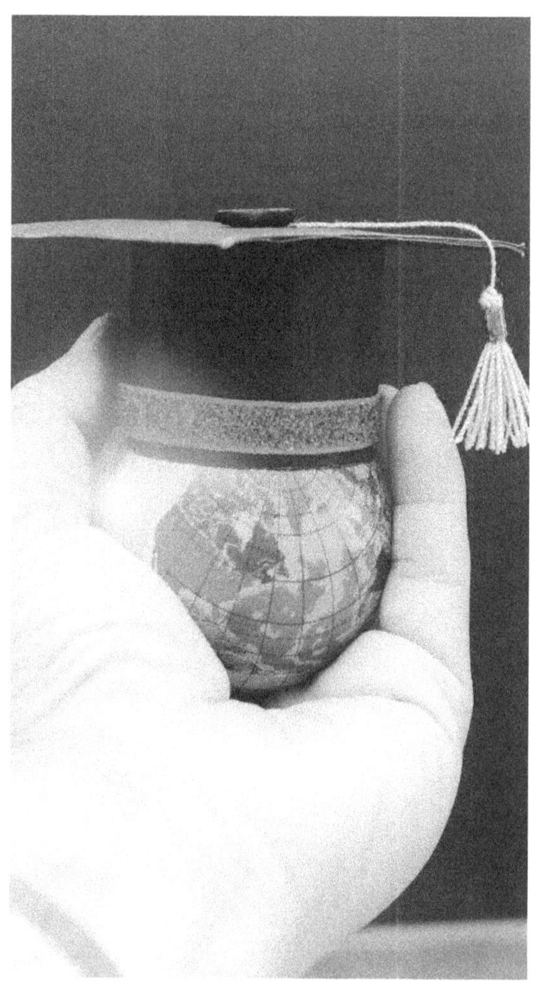

To the Student

When being schooled
in secular learning,
don't let go of the iron rod.

The philosophies of man
would have you turning
away from the mysteries of God.

Service to Others

Life is largely worthless
unless given shape and form and
purpose,

and there is no greater purpose than
that of helping our fellowman

87.5
LW
MHz
108
TUNING
POWER
VOLUME
MIN
MAX

Getting in Tune

Visions of glory
      disseminate across the land,
but we will not see or
hear them blasting

until we tune our souls
      to the same waveband
on which the Holy Ghost
is broadcasting.

And lead
nto tempt
but deliv
evil.
the

The Lord's Prayer (and Ours)

Amid a world
of gross malfeasance
in trouble and turmoil
and momentous upheaval,

peaceful comfort
and re-assurance
are found in the words,
"Deliver us from evil."

Think Celestial

To all who are
Heavenward pressing,
here's a bone
on which to gnaw;

if you desire
celestial blessings,
you must live by
celestial law.

Wake Up

Something fundamental
in our basic makeup
will, sooner or later,
cause us to wake up
and turn us toward our Creator.

Receiving Light

We wait on the Lord
to receive truth and light
and we find
our situation is bleak,

for, in fact, it's the Lord
who is waiting on us
to be worthy
of the light that we seek.

Life and Love

This truth I know
to be supernal—

like life itself,
love is eternal.

Paying the Price

This is true
in a
temporal or
a spiritual store—

you only
receive
what you're willing
to pay for.

He is Aware

This is *His* kingdom,
this is *His* plan;
He is aware
of who *I* am.

Complete Conversion

If you want your
conversion and commitment
to be complete,

you must be more than
a card-carrying member
with a tithing receipt.

Forewarned

God warns us through
the voice of tempests,
earthquakes, and seas heaving
beyond their bounds.

Do we hear His voice
in our lives today
and do we recognize
those warning sounds?

SIN

Much Too Big

The heavy
weight of sin

is much too big
of a burden.

Results

All of us will
one day realize

the results of how
we lived our lives.

I hope you have enjoyed this little volume.

Please post an honest 5-star review on a book site where you have posting privileges. You could mention which grook was your favorite.

If you found this book enjoyable, inspirational, educational, or enlightening, please tell your friends about it.

About the Author

Bill Wylson is the author of over 50 published works on family values, religious issues, and religious education. His work has appeared in *The Ensign, This People, The New Era, Liberty Magazine, Success,* and others.

Bill graduated from the *Columbia School of Broadcasting* in Hollywood, CA, as a commercial copywriter. He wrote trade journal ads for a major advertising agency in Los Angeles and public service announcements for a Los Angeles television station.

He has served as a volunteer Board Member of *Advocates of Single Parent Youth, Special Fun Games for the Disabled*, and on the Boards of Arts and Theater Councils. He has also served on Advisory Committees for the *Volunteer Center of Los Angeles* and on the *United Way Government Affairs Committee*.

Bill Wylson lives in Salt Lake City, Utah.

Other Books by Bill Wylson

Give Place in Your Heart:
31 Promises from the Book of Mormon

All of us are familiar with Moroni's promise that Christ will manifest the truth of the Book of Mormon to us by the power of the Holy Ghost. This is just one of many promises the Lord has made regarding the Book of Mormon.

The concepts presented in this book encourage personal growth and self-reflection. By recognizing the conditions attached to each promise from the Lord, readers can make positive changes that enhance their spiritual character.

In *Give Place in Your Heart*, Bill Wylson outlines 31 promises, with their attendant blessings and conditions, that the Lord would love to bestow upon you.

A New Earth
The Core Cause of Climate Change

Climate change is real.

There really should be no question about it. However, polarized views about climate issues stretch from the causes and cures for climate change to issues of trust or skepticism in climate scientists and their research.

According to NASA: *"Climate change is one of the most complex issues facing us today. It involves many dimensions—science, economics, society, politics and moral and ethical questions—and is a global problem, felt on local scales, that will be around for decades and centuries to come."*

The only real question is: "What can we do about it?"

The answer might surprise you.

Latter-day Grooks
Volumes One, Two, and Three

Grooks were originally created by the Danish poet Piet Hein, (1905–1996) who wrote over 10,000 of them in both the Danish and English languages. A grook ('gruk' in Danish) is a form of short aphoristic poem or rhyming aphorism.

Literary experts suggest that the term 'gruk' is a compilation of the Danish words 'GRin and sUK', meaning to laugh and sigh. Grooks are multi-faceted and are meant to be spirit-building. They are often characterized by irony, paradox, brevity, precise use of language, rhythm, and rhyme.

In these volumes, Bill Wylson has attempted to cite the words and teachings from the Church of Jesus Christ of Latter-day Saints and to express their ideas in the form of latter-day grooks.

Three Minutes Eighteen Seconds:
A Prophet's Final Message to the World

Words are extremely powerful. Lord Byron poetically portrays this truth:

"But words are things, and a small drop of ink,
Falling like dew, upon a thought, produces
That which makes thousands, perhaps millions, think."

Three Minutes Eighteen Seconds examines three "small drops of ink" that are simultaneously extremely powerful words spoken by President Thomas S. Monson at the April 2017 General Conference, his final message to the people of this world.

Hieroglyphs, Golden Plates and Typos:

On the inside cover of his first leather-bound Book of Mormon, my father had written the following quotation from the prophet Joseph Smith:

"I told the brethren that the Book of Mormon was the most correct of any book on earth, and the keystone of our religion, and a man would get nearer to God by abiding by its precepts, than by any other book."

Directly below this quote, my father had compiled a list of scriptures labeled: "Mistakes in the Book of Mormon."

Committing his writings to the future reader, Moroni candidly and apologetically acknowledged: *"And if there be faults they be the faults of a man. But behold, we know no fault."* How did my father have the audacity to make a list of mistakes in the Book of Mormon? To better understand these 'corrections' in the Book of Mormon and how they testify to its truthfulness and authenticity, we need to understand the process involved in making plates of ore and the method for inscribing on them.

Elder Hammond and the Inspector

"You know, there's a word to describe someone who won't even bother to meet you at the bus station. It starts with an 'O' or, I don't know, maybe a 'C' or something. I think it's C-a—. No, I've lost it."

Elder Hammond was a freckled-face, shy sort of bumpkin from some rural farm town in Kansas. He was awkward and withdrawn. Even in his white shirt and tie, he reminded you of the type of kid you'd see in denim coveralls, wearin' a straw hat and chompin' on a thin blade of grass whilst irrigatin' the lower forty.

I knew nothing about Elder Hammond's personal life. He was just a simple, quiet, humble boy, determined and dedicated. He had no delusions of grandeur, just a desire to serve. Perhaps more than any missionary, Elder Hammond had a purity of spirit and an altruistic motivation in ministering. I pitied him. I think he actually believed he could make a difference.

The Manger on the Mantle
A Christmas Tale based on Two True Stories

The Manger on the Mantle recounts the tragic life of Mark Spencer, a man raised in a small town who somehow becomes very lost in the massive city of Los Angeles. He didn't become geographically lost; he became spiritually lost.

As his family falls apart and his world collapses, Mark realizes just how tainted his life has become. He has strayed so far from the innocence of his youth, and now he fears he may never find his way back.

That's when Mark meets Marvin, a sockless, root-beer-float-toting ex-hippie. Together, they journey the road to Bethlehem as they ponder the purpose of a birth in a lowly manger.

The Manger on the Mantle is a beautiful story of hope and redemption and the joyous possibility of being given a second chance.

The Greatest Thing in the World
The Restored Gospel Version

In 1883, Henry Drummond, a Scottish scientist-evangelist, presented a powerful essay on 1st Corinthians 13, Paul's chapter on charity and the pure love of Christ. The "Restored Gospel Version" brings the added perspective of modern-day revelation to a timeless classic.

Drummond's message of charity is as vital and essential today as when he first delivered it: *"The words which all of us shall one day hear sound not of theology, but of life, not of churches and saints but of the hungry and the poor, not of creeds and doctrines, but of shelter and clothing, not of Bibles and prayerbooks but of cups of cold water offered in the name of Christ."*

The essay contains three parts: The Contrast, The Analysis, and The Defense. Drummond's simple yet profound message is short, but it is a message that can and should alter your life. The Reverend Dwight Moody said he had *"never heard anything so beautiful."*

The Greatest Thing in the World is a book that belongs in everyone's library.